Ria Money Transfer: a transnational compai
clientele
Ibrahim Sirkeci & Anett Condick-Brough

OFF PRINT
Volume 4 | Number 1 | May 2016

CASE STUDY: Ria Money Transfer: a transnational
company for a transnational clientele
Ibrahim Sirkeci & Anett Condick-Brough

41-58

TRANSNATIONAL MARKETING JOURNAL

ISSN: 2041-4684
e-ISSN: 2041-4692

Ria Money Transfer: a transnational company for a transnational

clientele by Ibrahim Sirkeci & Anett Condick-Brough

First Published in 2016 by TRANSNATIONAL PRESS LONDON in the
United Kingdom, 12 Ridgeway Gardens, London, N6 5XR, UK.
www.tplondon.com

Paperback

ISBN: 978-1-910781-24-1

Cover Design: Nihal Yazgan @nihalidea.com

May 2016
Volume: 4, **No**: 1, pp. 41 – 58
ISSN: 2041-4684
e-ISSN: 2041-4692
TransnationalMarket.com

TRANSNATIONAL
MARKETING
JOURNAL

Article history: Received 15 December 2015; accepted 22 April 2016

CASE STUDY
Ria Money Transfer: a transnational company for a transnational clientele[1]

Ibrahim Sirkeci[Υ]
Anett Condick-Brough[±]

Abstract

This case study looks at the development of a money transfer company in a dynamic and fast changing market. Transnational nature of the business as well as profiles of customers are emphasised. Ria Money Transfer is part of the Euronet, US based parent company. Aspiring to become the most progressive company in the sector, Ria deals with customers with backgrounds from all over the world. This is also reflected in the work force of the company. Operating in distinct environments, businesses are not only concerned with a multicultural body of customers, agents and clients but also multiple economic, political, technological environments with a large number of small and big competitors. This case study alludes to the questions about the key drivers of success for a transnational company with such complex web of markets, consumers, clients and competitors. Company information, direct quotes from representatives and media are used to illustrate aspects of the business and markets.

Keywords: *Ria Money Transfer; remittances; agents; transnational strategy; transnational consumers*

Baker Street

On an unusually cold day in March, we received a very warm welcome at Ria Money Transfer's offices in Baker Street, London. On a mission our world famous fictional resident Sherlock Holmes would not dare to take, we began our investigation of this relatively well-known money transfer company. Marcela Gonzalez, Managing Director for the UK and Ireland and Victor Salamanca, Marketing and New Projects Director, greeted our team of four with big smiles. This is pretty reflective of Ria's humble beginnings which started in 1987 in New York City, with a single storefront in the city to help migrants send money back home. This entrepreneurial altruism has been emulated by many money

[1] We would like to thank *Ria Money Transfer* management team for their support by providing information and allowing us to visit and interview their staff in their offices.

[Υ] Prof Dr Ibrahim Sirkeci, Ria Professor of Transnational Studies and Marketing, Regent's Centre for Transnational Studies, Faculty of Business and Management, Regent's University London, UK. E-mail: sirkecii@regents.ac.uk.

[±] Dr Anett Condick-Brough, Research Assistant, Regent's Centre for Transnational Studies, Regent's University London, United Kingdom. E-mail: cbrougha@regents.ac.uk.

transfer companies ever since, with over 100 companies emerging in the sector worldwide.

Ria, the world's third largest consumer-to-consumer money transfer company, was acquired in 2007 by Euronet, a leading electronic payments provider, after an agreement with the Los Angeles based Ria Envia Inc. in late 2006. Following the acquisition, Michael J. Brown, CEO and Founder of Euronet, said "*Ria, through its family of brands, has a compelling core business in the traditional money transfer corridor between the US and Latin America, together with its European and Asian presence*" and emphasised the transnational potential for growth through substantial "*geographic, economic and relationship synergies ... positioning Euronet to provide remittance services across many markets around the world*". On a celebratory note, Juan C. Bianchi, the CEO of Ria Envia, underlined the cross-border advantages: "*aside from the obvious market opportunities, we believe the Ria and Euronet operating philosophies and cultures will fit together nicely.*" After eight years, it seems this expectation has been exceeded, as Ria continues to grow with Euronet as its parent company.

Euronet defines Ria Money Transfer in terms of a mediator service: "*Ria initiates transfers through a network of sending agents and company-owned stores located throughout North America, Latin America, Europe and Asia-Pacific, as well as online from the United States at www.riamoneytransfer. com*"[2]. They also have operations in Africa and according to Sian Bennett, PR & Communication Director at the company, as of December 31, 2015 Ria's global network spanned over 147 countries with services in more than 292,000 locations with growth that shows no signs of slowing. On June 22, 2015, the company announced the acquisition of IME, a leading Malaysian money transfer provider. IME generated about USD $40 million in revenue in 2014 and enjoys an international network of 75,000 payout locations worldwide.[3] Over time, Ria has grown into a major challenger of the market leader, Western Union. Indeed, in certain money remittance corridors such as US-Mexico, Ria has become the market leader. By 2012, Ria had reached over 20,000 payout locations in Latin America, essentially making it the largest single money transfer network in the region.[4]

In addition to money transfer services, Ria offers Currency Exchange, Mobile Top-up, Pre-Paid Debit Cards, Check Cashing and Remittance Payout at Euronet ATMs in certain countries around the world. Ria's mission is to be the most progressive money transfer company globally, offering service excellence and the most reliable and competitive remittance payment services to its customers.

Hence, you can imagine our surprise when Sophia[5] told us during the interview we conducted at Ria's Baker Street Offices, that "*it is not about the money*

---

[2] Euronet (2015).

[3] See http://globenewswire.com/news-release/2015/06/22/746418/0/en/Ria-Acquires-Malaysian-Money-Transfer-Provider-IME.html.

[4] Orozco M., & Yansura, J., & Slooten, B. (2013).

[5] Please note some names have been altered to ensure confidentiality.

itself'. So what is it about then? We know that within just a few years, Ria grew to generate about 25 per cent of Euronet's revenues globally. The number of completed transactions by Ria rose from 19.1 million transactions in 2009 to 35.2 million transactions in 2013 when they reported a network with 22 sending and 136 receiving countries[6].

Before the acquisition of the California headquartered Ria, Euronet set-up shop in Hungary in 1996 and later moved to Delaware, USA in August 2001.[7] The international expansion of the business is reflected in the fact that by 2012, only 23 per cent of sales were recorded in its home country, the US; Euronet reported $1.66 billion in annual revenues through processing 2.5 billion transactions in 2014[8]. Due to their efforts in lowering the cost of remittances, Ria has gained greater recognition within the money transfer industry and financial sector. As mentioned above, the growth also arises from new acquisitions by Ria within the money transfer sector.

The total volume of recorded remittances is estimated to exceed $601 billion worldwide by the end of 2015 a significant increase from 2012, as reported in the World Bank study.[9] This volume exceeds the GDPs of most countries around the globe with more than half directed towards developing countries. It is estimated that the number of informal remittances made equates to between 35% and 75% of transactions made in the recorded remittance market,[10] hence the potential consumer-to-consumer money transfer market is much larger than what is actually on record.

There has been significant growth in the volume of remittances received in developing countries since the 1980s; from less than $75 billion to over $451 billion in 2015. Even during the financial crisis, remittances have proven to be resilient in most parts of the world.[11] Remittance sending practices date back to 700 AD China, where tea merchants were given remittance certificates by city tax offices, mainly to avoid the risks of carrying money while travelling back to their home cities.[12] Today, one can talk of similar risks, but improvements in money transfer services and the reduced costs of sending remittances, have contributed to the rapid growth of the market.

Ria, with its low cost model (Table 1) has gained market share rapidly, as well as driving down the costs of money transfer for those beneficiaries in countries of origin and destination countries. The average cost of a remittance transfer is estimated to be approximately 2-10 per cent of the amount of the transfer. Remittance companies such as Ria unburden remittance senders by bundling the funds at origin and unbundling at the destination, hence individual

---

[6] Euronet (2013).
[7] Euronet (2011).
[8] Euronet (2014).
[9] Sirkeci, I., & Cohen, J.H., & Ratha, D. (2012).
[10] Freund, C., & Spatafora, N. (2005).
[11] Sirkeci, I., & Cohen, J.H. & Ratha, D. (2012).
[12] Buencamino, L., & Gorbunov, S. (2002).

bank transfer costs are reduced significantly. This cost reduction in transactions has been promoted by many scholars and industry leaders, including the World Bank's Dilip Ratha. In his 2014 TED talk, Ratha urged governments to relax regulations on remittances and said *"small remittances are not money laundering"* as people only send about $200 per month.[13] Another important message in his talk was that remittances were *"dollars wrapped with care"*. It is not only about money. But if it is really not just about the money, then we should investigate the topic further and hope that as a result, our efforts would make even Sherlock Holmes nod with delight.

Table 1: Top ten firms: Cost of sending £120 from the UK to Ghana, Q4 2015

Firm	Product	Fee	Exchange Rate Margin (%)	Total Cost Percent (%)	Total Cost (GBP)
Azimo	Online	1.00	0.59	1.42	1.70
Ria Money Transfer	Cash to cash and credit/debit card service	4.80	-0.21	3.79	4.55
WorldRemit	Online	2.99	1.64	4.13	4.96
Sigue Money Transfers	Cash to cash	5.00	0.75	4.91	5.89
First African Remittances	Cash to cash	6.00	-0.06	4.94	5.93
Samba Money Transfers	Cash to cash	6.00	0.05	5.05	6.06
Small World FS-Express Funds	Cash to cash	6.00	0.08	5.08	6.10
Unity Link	Cash to cash, Online and Cash to account services	7.00	0.14	5.97	7.16
PayAfrique.com	Online	6.99	0.70	6.52	7.82
Lebara	Prepaid card	9.70	0.36	8.45	10.14

Source: The World Bank, http://remittanceprice.worldbank.org

Ria's customers

Ria prides itself on shortening the distance between families and their loved ones through their world class money transfer service. Their stated aim is to offer the simplest, most reliable and friendly money transfer service. Talking to Ria's team made one thing clear: compared to traditional bank transfer channels, Ria targets consumers with very different backgrounds. To further

---

[13] Ratha, D. (2014).

understand the company's customer base, we need to differentiate between sending and receiving countries. The former can be identified as a country where the majority of money transfers are initiated while nations that tend to be beneficiaries of transfers are called receiving countries.

The firm identified a particular need among migrant or ethnic[14] minority communities. Many have moved to sender countries such as the UK or US to establish a better life and are keen to help those left behind in the countries of origin. Ria recognised that these people have very special circumstances that cannot be characterised as static or one-way. The key element is that they are true transnationals, maintaining social and economic links with their country of origin, whilst mobile and ready to move to another country if their needs are met better elsewhere. In many cases these individuals send and receive money in several countries where they have taken residence (i.e. countries they have moved to and lived in for a substantial period of time in the past), where they have established friendships, acquaintances and business relationships. This means creating a very dynamic and complex set of personal, financial and economic networks through which transfers occur, financial or other.

This is where transnational money transfer and Ria come into the picture. Ria's transnational strategy aims to achieve lower costs and prices for its customers, along with accessibility, reliability and quality. Thus it offers an easy and affordable way to meet the demands of migrants and ethnic minorities to facilitate sending money to support people and communities left behind. As a result, millions of people at the lower level of income scale – usually the elderly, children and other relatives of migrants – benefit from and rely on remittances that are sent back home.

Vulnerability can be detected not just on the receiving end of these transfers, though. The senders are in an exposed position too, living in a foreign country with significantly less knowledge of the formal and informal institutions now regulating their everyday lives. An additional constraining factor is the language barrier. For example, if we look at the case of Great Britain – although it is difficult to record the exact number of people having little command of English language – once it was estimated to be around 4.5 million.[15] There is also a notable disparity amongst the different linguistic groups in terms of language skills. The survival level English knowledge is known to be higher among Chinese than Bengali speaking individuals in the UK, for example[16].

The lack of knowledge of a particular system, paired with language difficulties, mean less familiarity and trust in traditional channels; in many cases this results in being underbanked or even unbanked (i.e. being unable to access banking system). Money transfer networks often find their clients among these

---

[14] We use this term defined as: 'in government research minority ethnic groups are differentiated based on a combination of categories including 'race', skin colour, national and regional origins, and language'. [Office for National Statistics (2003).]

[15] Data is based on calculation based on Schellekens, P. (2001).

[16] The Working Group on ESOL (2000).

underbanked and unbanked around the world, and not necessarily in developing countries. If we think about it, economic interactions take place under uncertain conditions, with asymmetric and incomplete information. It is the institutional system that ensures the ex post fulfilment and enforceability of ex ante commitments,[17] which fundamentally determines the options and limitations of the market actors. If we do not trust in the formal or informal enforceability of commitments, we simply do not initiate economic transactions. In other words, if we do not trust that a faulty jumper can be returned and fully refunded, we do not buy it in the first place – or in the example of our Case Study, we will not attempt to transfer our hard-earned money to a different country if we cannot make sure it reaches its destination.

Ria located a niche market, but one with many limitations. It incorporated highly mobile, vulnerable individuals lacking trust, but who were also in need of a reliable and inexpensive money transfer option. Some of the 250 million international migrants[18] around the world and their families, who remain in the countries of origin, constitute the typical clients of Ria and other remittance service providers. The crucial question is how to access this market which is so fragmented and often spans across national borders. One does not merely help Mexican immigrants in the US to send money back to Mexico, or Turks in Germany to send money back to Turkey; there are many other flows. Mexicans also send money to their families within the US, while some Turks send money from Germany to the UK or France. One should also note that despite the fact that the bulk of remittances are sent to developing countries, about a third – or nearly \$200 billion worth of remittances every year – head to advanced economies such as the UK, US, and Germany.

Nevertheless, connecting with customers is a key for success which Ria manages to achieve and naturally, they pursue customer-specific communication and marketing campaigns. For example, in 2014, they ran a campaign with a special offer to their Muslim customers, offering a trip, with the tagline: *Ria takes you to Mecca!* As one might expect, this slogan was translated and used in eight different languages. However, Ria mainly connects to customers through its local agent network, which is easily accessible among ethnic communities in Europe and America.

What makes Ria's agents and services different?

The difficulty in reaching this sector stems from the fact that people generally prefer to interact and form communities with individuals with similar values, while often creating or moving into ethnic or immigrant enclaves. This is partly because immigrants typically leave their social networks behind when they move to another country which can lead to a sense of insecurity[19] until

---

[17] North, D. C. (1991).
[18] The World Bank estimation.
[19] See Sirkeci, I. (2009).

they settle into a new network in their destination country, which logically involves people of the same background. Therefore, migrants tend to favour tradespeople – and money transfer agents – who are closer to them culturally and socially[20].

That is precisely what Ria seems to have put at the focus of its marketing strategy: Building bridges with migrants and ethnic minorities through agents selected from local communities. They developed a business model partnering with many local small and medium enterprises (SMEs) as their certified agents. They were aware that these small companies had special needs and thus offered a

Photo: Ria Money Transfer Team at meeting (from Ria Blog, Available at: http://riafinancialblog.com/2014/11/27/ria-talks-innovation-and-technology-at-global-money-transfer-summit/

risk-free opportunity to increase revenues with no need for upfront investment. It would be fair to say the business model worked well considering Ria currently has more than 292,000 paying and receiving agents in 147 countries worldwide[21]. For the most part, becoming a Ria Agent is often a secondary activity, initially to help out with existing business expenses, e.g. rent and wages, and as a means of attracting more trade[22].

Ria supplies its Agents with start-up capital, revolving credit and business know-how and support, including training, marketing materials and a customer service always ready to help at the other end of the phone. As Rodney from Ria's Baker Street offices said *"the technical requirement is just a computer with internet access – that's it"*.

These elements were vital for Ria's success, as they made it easy for their potential partners to open up their businesses to a new avenue of revenue with this reliable turnkey solution. Ria, relying on a large multicultural workforce, who have been movers themselves, has an instinct to understand its clients and agents.

The company understood early on that *"what the customer looks for is value for money"* explained Karl at Ria's Baker Street Office. Therefore, creating a secure, fairly-priced and fast alternative to traditional bank transfers allowed Ria to grow at a swift pace, to become the third largest money transfer company

---

[20] Akerlof, G. A. (1997) and Hodosi, A. (2012).
[21] Data correct as at Dec 31, 2015.
[22] Ria website: http://www.riafinancial.com

globally today. Fair commissions paid to agents and a low-cost alternative to other more expensive channels have been crucial to this growth. Ria's connection with immigrant communities and ethnic minorities did not just help build a sales network, but simultaneously created its organic marketing channels. Services offered by co-ethnics known through social networks help build trust and spread the word. It is possible that the company benefited from these social networks which are advantageous for word of mouth marketing.

Forming multilingual, multicultural teams on the way to transnational success

What really helped both customers and agents was the trust offered by Ria – a reliable and financially secure company. Everybody wants security against risks. It is important for customers who do not want to lose their hard-earned money, while agents avoid the headache of having to manage and finance both an efficient money transfer system and customer service. The business model can also drive costs down, while ensuring a consistently high level of quality service in this transnational sector of money transfers.

Naturally, transnational strategies require transnational teams. This is why staff profile is one of the three components of the United Nations Trade Conference's transnationality index, along with assets and sales. Ria understands the value in having a transnational staff portfolio as part of the service marketing mix. Clearly their clients are from transnational population segments: Ethnic and immigrant groups in wealthier countries, and their friends, families and networks around the world. Hence the need for Ria to speak the languages of these customers and understand their cultures.

In Ria, from the top managerial team to the 287,000 money transfer locations[23], a variety in cultural backgrounds is reflected. Ria's CEO & President, Juan Bianchi, is from Chile and educated in the US; fellow countryman Sebastian Plubins, Ria's EMEA & South Asia Managing Director, has lived in Santiago, London, Madrid, and Geneva, and is a truly transnational mobile professional like many other colleagues on Ria's payroll.

Ria's Agents are often found in ethnic concentration areas reflecting the main money transfer destinations. These agents are usually well-connected in their local communities and therefore it is easy and convenient for their customers to find them.

Ria has over 60 nationalities on the payroll and about 55 per cent of its over 3,000 employees are based overseas, i.e. outside of the US, where the headquarters are based. Nevertheless, the transnational profile of staff does not end there. In nearly every location where Ria has offices based it employs multi-ethnic teams. For example, you may find 2 Colombians, 1 Nigerian and 1 Ivorian (from the Ivory Coast) working together in a small team in their London office, supported by other teams including Pakistanis and Senegalese, all

---

[23] Ria website: https://riafinancial.com data correct as at Sept 30, 2015.

representing the major markets the company serves. The advantage is obvious, as Tomasz tells it: *"We have different faces to different communities. I know how Polish react because I am Polish. This is very important for Polish customers"*. Hence, it is not simply the language, but both a linguistic and cultural understanding of the specific community that is being served.

Some support services and telebanking are built with a multilingual perspective at Ria offices around Europe and the Americas. The teams are equipped with employees who are speakers of many languages including Tagalog, Spanish, Filipina, French, Polish, and Portuguese. One of the Ria managers we met in London was well aware of the need when he told us that *"if our main country is China, we need to speak Chinese to penetrate into the country"*. Furthermore, in global cities such as London, ethnic concentration areas seemingly evolved to see what we may call an 'ethnic group oriented business strategy'. For example, the Baker Street office serves a certain group of customers sending remittances predominantly to a few countries with similar characteristics. This is more or less true for their 1,500 other payment locations across the UK. It enables the company to break the disadvantage of large differences between markets and to spread trust within local communities. For example, in some countries they organise different events and advertisements with the aim of creating marketing hotspots. In other countries, such as the UK, they *"don't need to explain what Ria is"*, Ahmed points out, because the company is so well-known among the ethnic and migrant communities.

Transnational workforce for transnational expansion

When we met Halil Keskin at a money transfer conference in Istanbul, Turkey in May 2015, he was excited about his new move. Ria established themselves permanently in Turkey when they opened an office in Levent, a business quarter of Istanbul. Ria's transnational expansion strategy is seemingly based on transnational consumer geography and transnational relocation of resources. Mr Keskin, a German national of Turkish origin, was a star talent transfer to Ria Money Transfer from rival Western Union in 2014. He is familiar with both sides of Turkish culture, German Turks and Turks in Turkey. Germany has been the main destination for migrants from Turkey since the 1961 bilateral labour exchange agreement between the two countries. Keskin is a perfect candidate, a Ruhr University Bochum educated Turk from Germany with roots in central Anatolia. Ria has already added around 4,500 payout points in Turkey. The transnational team, or global team shipped from Germany now strives to gain a firm footing in Turkey's dynamic market which is full of opportunity for growth in the remittances sector due to the arrival of large numbers of migrants from Syria and beyond since 2011. Turkey has been a stable receiver of remittances since the 1970s, and today the country is developing a sending market too, in line with increasing immigration. Until recently, Western Union and Moneygram, the top two market leaders, were dominating this market.

As many current and former employees testify, Ria is "*a great international company to work for with dynamic, multicultural, great and interesting people from around the world.*" Despite relatively lower pay scales compared to other market leaders, many talented people form a transnational workforce at Ria's service network. Like the three floors in Baker Street's London office or the Alcobendas office in Madrid, Ria may resemble a model United Nations.

In June 2015, Ria officially entered the Malaysian market through the acquisition of IME, a leading Malaysian money transfer provider. In June 2015, Reuters reported this as a strategic expansion, saying that the deal "*provides Ria with immediate entry into the important Asian and Middle East send markets and will allow Ria to more quickly replicate the success achieved in the U.S. and Europe over the last decade.*"[24] This can be considered another broken chain in exclusivity agreements that Ria is wrestling with as they continue entering new markets. Together South Asia and the Middle East comprise the countries with the largest remittances sending and receiving corridors.

Transnational market entry

There are many known ways to enter new markets: franchising, acquisition and subsidiaries are to name but a few. "Diaspora market entry" and "transnational market entry" are new strategies many companies may benefit from. Diaspora marketing is simply looking at exploiting the opportunities arising from the presence of immigrant communities in developed economies. Bangladeshi brands entering the UK market or Turkish brands entering into Germany are typical examples one can examine. Immigrants and their descendants create attractive market opportunities as they often concentrate in certain locations making them easier to segment and target (Sirkeci, 2013). Companies from the countries of origin, such as Turkey, gain advantage as they are familiar with these consumers from a previous location and more importantly they speak the same language to which diaspora communities are receptive.

Consumers tend to seek the brands they have been loyal to until they are frustrated with the search and move on to a substitute. This is a crucial period for businesses to retain their customers. It is also a small window of opportunity to enter a new market following the migrating loyal customers, although there can be a second opportunity later on through appealing to nostalgic consumer taste. This type of market entry is called "Diaspora market entry"[25] or "Transnational Market Entry"[26]. Nevertheless, the latter also considers two-way internationalisation opportunities. The presence of diaspora communities opens up new prospects for companies in the host nations too. Hence when, for example, Pakistani brands make enter the UK market, British brands may

---

[24] Reuters http://www.reuters.com/article/idUSnGNX4L4g5Y+1d1+GNW20150622
[25] Kumar and Steenkamp (2013).
[26] Sirkeci (2013).

benefit from their experience with Pakistani consumers in the UK and subsequently move into markets in Pakistan. Ria's repatriation of Halil Keskin from Germany to Istanbul is a prime example of the company benefiting from Keskin's experience of working with Turkish clients in Germany, as well as utilising a valuable human resource with knowledge of the market in Turkey itself. This type of transnational market entry would perhaps be called "reverse diaspora marketing" by Kumar and Steenkamp.

As a result of its transnational strategy and the multicultural team behind it, Ria is able to reach out to many vulnerable communities and feel that they make a real impact by offering a relatively lower cost money transfer which left a few dollars extra available to those families in the (often poorer) countries of origin. In extreme poverty, which many poorer countries suffer from, every cent counts. They support countless ethnic entrepreneurs through the provision of start-up capital to become Ria Agents and by offering a great alternative to generate more revenue. The additional income helps many small companies in securing their employees' jobs and providing added certainty for their families. Thanks to the worldwide network of agents the company has gradually built, it is easier for immigrants and ethnic minorities to send remittances home and thus improve the lives of their loved ones left behind.

These money transfers do not just create additional businesses in the developed world, but also benefit local firms in receipt of the remitted money. There is a positive spill over effect for the receiving agents as the beneficiaries visiting their stores create a potential extra customer base. As SMEs generate more than 50 per cent of employment worldwide according to the World Bank, they work as a catalyst for economic growth. Yet, in many regions financial services are under-developed and SMEs are struggling to gain access to them. Consequently, remittances are of great importance in these cases, fuelling economies with additional funds.

At times, the total received remittances can constitute even 30 or 40% of a country's GDP. Table 2 displays Ria's contribution to GDP through money transfers originated via the company in 2013. The largest impact can be detected in El Salvador, where the level of Ria remittances reached almost 3% of the country's GDP. This small but densely populated country depends heavily on transnational money transfer and benefits from it on a daily basis.

Table 2. Estimated percentage of GDP represented by Ria remittances in 2013	
COUNTRY	**GDP %**
El Salvador	2.91%
The Gambia	2.07%
Comoros	1.76%
Senegal	1.22%
Honduras	1.07%
Guatemala	1.06%
Togo	1.01%
Source: Compiled by authors	

Even in the case of Togo that had an estimated total of $7.348 billion GDP in 2013, we can observe that Ria's contribution was significant considering the one per cent constituted $73.48 million in total. However, the benefit of remittances cannot be measured in a purely monetary sense. It has created and maintained channels between communities in the receiving and sending countries. It has allowed migrants and ethnic minorities to stay in touch with their roots and to help out those back home in urgent need. Companies like Ria promote a new era that goes beyond globalisation – true transnationalism.[27]

Ria's transnational challenges

Naturally, there were and still are many obstacles to expansion and new market entry, as in many countries the sector is saturated. For example, according to HMRC, 3,522 MT businesses including agents are registered with approximately 48,000 premises across the UK, making the country one of the toughest markets to penetrate within the money transfer sector. Ria currently runs a network of over 1,260 agents nationwide[28] and is rapidly increasing its market share in the UK. India, Bangladesh, Pakistan and Poland, among others, are top key corridors for the UK market. These countries also represent the key corridors where Ria is currently enjoying the fastest growth. It should be noted that Ria was the top money transfer company reporting continuous significant growth from 2008 to 2011, at the peak of the global financial crisis.[29]

Changing regulations and tougher control measures are posing a challenge to those small companies without robust control systems. Market penetration is always a challenge. However, various arrangements and agreements between governments and regulators in the past giving the market leaders a privileged position are making it even tougher for challenger operators such as Ria. In this line of business, partnering with banks and improving the service while keeping the costs down is a winning -but a very difficult to achieve- strategy.

In 2012, Ria entered an agreement with Commercial Bank to make receiving money from families and friends abroad easier for Sri Lankans. Sanath Bandaranayake, the Bank's Deputy General Manager, said strategic ties with global players had made the Commercial Bank's provision in the area of remittances attractive for both remitters and their beneficiaries in Sri Lanka. He also added that "Commercial Bank remains committed to further strengthening its partner network, especially in areas with a large Sri Lankan expatriate population."[30]

These markets with established cultures of international migration and sizeable diaspora populations are important for money transfer businesses. Similarly, Ria signed a correspondent agent agreement with the First Bank in

---

[27] For more on this topic please see: Sirkeci, I. (2013) and Kumar, N., & Steenkamp, J. B. E. (2013).
[28] http://riafinancial.com
[29] Orozco, M., & Yansura, J., & Slooten, B. (2013).
[30] Economy Watch (2012).

Nigeria, one of the top ten remittance receiving countries globally, according to the World Bank.[31] Earlier in 2012, Ria made advances in Mexico by signing an agreement with Grupo Elektra which was welcomed by Mr Brown, CEO of Euronet, as "a mutually beneficial, exciting and long-term relationship".[32] This move increased Ria's penetration by 11% in Mexico, another major country with a large expatriate population. Such a global reach resulted in Ria having 82 per cent of its assets located outside the US.

However, there are strong obstacles on the road to growth. As Ria's Managing Director Sebastian Plubins has been highlighting at various events, there are legal battles to be fought, especially on exclusivity agreements between money transfer companies and governments.[33] According to UK newspaper the Guardian, *"two companies are alleged to be restricting entry into the remittances marketplace in Africa"*.[34] Apparently the recipients in poorest countries are paying the largest bill for remittances: Sending $1000 to Africa costs $124 compared to a $78 world average and a $65 average in South Asia. Ismail Ahmed, Chief Executive of the online money transfer firm WorldRemit strongly claimed that the two market leaders *"are ubiquitous and that dominance has allowed them to dictate terms in many markets – in some cases imposing punitively high fees"*.[35] While even Kofi Annan, the former president of the UN, noted that remittance fees to Africa were "unethically expensive". Spokespersons from the two companies under fire refuted the allegations. Carl-Olav Scheible, MoneyGram's executive vice-president for Europe and Africa, rejected the duopoly allegation pointing to their share in African remittances market which is less than 15%. Accordingly high fees are due to the costs of compliance, customer service, operations, technology and global funding and settlement. Similar cost factors were cited by a Western Union spokeswoman too.[36]

An equally large challenge to the exclusivity agreements is the problem of the current heavy-handed and equally unnecessary scrutiny over small amounts of money sent by immigrants which many leaders in the sector have long argued need to be scrapped. Also, improving financial literacy could hold many advantages for money transfers[37].

The future for Ria Money Transfer

Ria Money Transfer is a growing and successful financial services company, anticipating the future delivery of user- friendly, convenient, digital financial services across various channels including web, mobile, and strategic

---

[31] Business Wire (2012a).
[32] Business Wire (2012b).
[33] Sebastian Plubins spoke at *Global Forum on Remittances and Development (GFRD)* which took place in Milan, Italy, June 16-19, 2015.
[34] Guardian (2014).
[35] Guardian (2014).
[36] Guardian (2014).
[37] Sirkeci, I. (2016).

partnerships/distribution. These digital capabilities are the key to Ria's future success as the transnationally connected world is becoming ever more internet savvy. Ria's vision of a service that is "always on", and available whenever, wherever and however people need it, serving underserved and mainstream customers anywhere on the globe, is the driving force for the company to address local needs while benefiting from global efficiencies as much as possible.

Located in Denver, USA, Ria Digital is a division within Ria focused on developing new ways to move money including linking the digital world to the physical "brick and mortar" world, and to provide choice and convenience to their customers. Ria Digital will lead the company into the fast-paced world of customer needs in the digital age, and they are looking for talented individuals to embrace this challenge, inspire a shared vision and drive the necessary accomplishment to meet these goals. Darren Bruce, who is in charge of Ria's digital operations which were set up in October 2012, says "*At Ria we pride ourselves on providing a fair price to consumers, it is very important to us, and the more costs that can be reduced in a transaction, the more savings that can be passed on to the customer.*"[38] Thus, Ria sees the importance of digital shift in money transfer sector and is taking cautious steps forward. The value added in digital services lies in the offer of stored value through mobile phone networks and increasingly ubiquitous smart phones as Bruce states:

> "*stored value / prepaid debit cards and mobile wallets empower the "un" or "under" banked, and allow these customers to take part in the ecommerce and/or digital financial services world. Specifically in regards to money transfer, these customers had no other choice in the past but to travel to a physical location with cash in order to send money to loved ones back home, now they can send from the palm of their hand easily and securely.*"

Ria is a company with modest moves and ambitions but is carefully listening to customers and innovating services. ATM based money transfer service via Euronet has been introduced in Poland. Customers can take the money sent to them from a large network of ATMs, without even using a bank card. While this is trialled in one country, the usual method of receiving money from post offices is maintained. The company needs to be careful about the variety of ways in which money is received in different countries and regions. However, there is a great deal of untapped opportunities in what may be called reverse diaspora marketing.

The word Ria may mean smile or mouth of a river in Spanish, while it means a narrow river inlet in English, but the brand name is short and sweet, a little like an art work, once out in the public everybody can attach a different meaning to it. This is why Nigerians, one of Ria's largest client communities, like the brand: it rhymes well with Nige-Ria. Or it can also rhyme with the popular

---

[38] Oak, C. (2014).

soccer chant in Hungary: "Ria, Ria, Hungaria!" Which one to choose, depends on your mood for the day.

Operating on a globalised and transnational platform requires open-mindedness and an excellent ability to embrace change. As we have seen through the case of Ria, corporations aiming to reach and impact transnational communities have to meet the global and local or "glocal"[39] needs of these consumers. Professor Lynda Gratton, Director of Future of Work Consortium, pointed out in an article in 2012,[40] that this high level of inter-connectedness around the globe generated a new playing field for corporations and employees. Due to the wide spread of technological developments people in remote areas are able to access high quality education and join a global work force online, while they are willing to move and remain mobile if opportunity presents itself elsewhere.

Part of the challenge to accommodate the needs of these consumers is that the scope of demand is constantly changing. For example, the 2008 financial crisis influenced remittances to such an extent that – after decades – Spain once again became a receiving country of money transfers. These volatile circumstances require close attention to each and every market of a transnational company. Those who would like to succeed need to constantly embrace change and adjust their business practices hand-in-hand with the transformations in the transnational world.

Spending a day at the Ria Baker Street offices left us with no doubt that they are doing just that. It was a great experience to gain an insight into this fast-growing and dynamic company, but being – or shall we rather say – trying to be Sherlock Holmes is not an easy task. We can only hope that Dr Watson would say: "Good job, well done."

---

[39] Sirkeci, I. (2014).
[40] Gratton, L. (2012).

Discussion Questions:

1) What is the case study about if not money?
2) What makes Ria transnational?
3) How does the company facilitate trust with its customers? What are the key elements of building trust? How could the company improve its current practice?
4) How did Ria enter new markets? What were the other market entry options available to the company?
5) What would be the key pillars of the ethical policy for Ria? What are the key concerns in the money transfer sector regarding ethics? How do regulations and strict rules affect the sector?
6) What are the digital challenges a brick and mortar company in this market faces?
7) What is diaspora marketing? How can you define reverse diaspora marketing?

References

Akerlof, G. A. (1997). Social Distance and Social Decisions. *Econometrics*, 65(5): 1005-1027.

Buencamino, L., & Gorbunov, S. (2002). Informal Money Transfer Systems: Opportunities and Challenges for Development Finance. *DESA Discussion Paper*, Paper No. 26, November 2002. Available at: http://www.un.org/esa/desa/papers/2002/esa02dp26.pdf?utm_source=OldRedirect&utm_medium=redirect&utm_campaign=OldRedirect

Business Wire (2012a). Ria Financial Services Announces Expansion in Africa with Partner FirstBank. June 2012. Available at: http://www.thefreelibrary.com/Ria+Financial+Services+Announces+Expansion+in+Africa+with+Partner...-a0293871702.

Business Wire (2012b). Ria Financial Services expands payout network in Mexico with Grupo Elektra. 15 March 2012. Available at: http://www.research-store.com/economywatch/News/ria_financial_services_expands_payout_network_in_mexico_with_grupo_elektra?productid=F1FA0B21-B97C-42B0-925B-EFB1F2E1CA0D.

Economy Watch (2012). Commercial Bank ties up with Ria Financial Services for remittances. Available at: http://www.research-store.com/economywatch/News/commercial_bank_ties_up_with_ria_financial_services_for_remittances?productid=858A917F-303B-4533-9147-C8C0AC5DEAF9.

Euronet (2011). Annual Report, Bringing currency to life. Available at www.euronetworldwide.com.

Euronet (2013). Annual Report 2013. Available at http://files.shareholder. com/downloads/EEFT/1146822221x0x744111/9F0DD756-0AA1-42F0-991C-396C6258D96D/2013_Annual_Report.pdf

Euronet (2014). Annual Report 2014. Available at http://files.shareholder.com/ downloads/EEFT/1146822221x0x820381/61807966-3F0B-49CA-8C72-AF18F9074BAC/Euronet_Annual_Report_Combined_2_FINAL.pdf

Euronet (2015). Ria Acquires Malaysian Money Transfer Provider IME. Euronet Press Release, June 22, 2015. http://ir.euronetworldwide.com/ releasedetail.cfm? ReleaseID=918968

Freund, C., & Spatafora, N. (2005). Remittances: Transaction Costs, Determinants, and Informal Flows. *World Bank Policy Research Working Paper*, No. 3704, September 2005.

Gratton, L. (2012). The globalisation of work - and people. Available at http://www.bbc.co.uk/news/business-19476254

Greif, A. (1993). Contract Enforceability and Economic Institutions in Early Trade: The Maghribi Traders' Coalition. *The American Economic Review*, 83(3): 525-548.

Guardian (2014). Global remittance industry choking billions out of developing world. *Guardian.* 18 August 2014. http://www.theguardian.com/global-development/ 2014/aug/18/global-remittance-industry-choking-billions-developing-world

Hodosi, A. (2012). The effects of immigration on the socio-economic landscape of the United Kingdom. *Eastern Journal of European Studies*, 3(2): 121-139.

Kumar, N., & Steenkamp, J. B. E. (2013). *Brand breakout: How emerging market brands will go global.* New York: Palgrave MacMillan.

North, D. C. (1991). Institutions. *Journal of Economic Perspectives*, 5(1): 97-112.

Oak, C. (2014). Ria Digital – Innovation in remittances within the Euronet group: Interview with Darren Bruce. *Shift Thought, Digital Money.* 19 November 2014, http://digitalmoney.shiftthought.co.uk/ria-digital-innovation-in-remittances-within-the-euronet-group/

Office for National Statistics (2003): Ethnic group statistics. For a guide for the collection and classification of ethnicity data, p.7. Available at http://www.ons.gov.uk]

Orozco M., & Yansura, J., & Slooten, B. (2013). A Long Road to Recovery: Market competition and the role of Western Union in the U.S.-Latin America and Caribbean corridor, http://www.thedialogue.org/

Ratha, D. (2014). The hidden force in global economics: sending money home. October, 2014. https://www.ted.com/talks/dilip_ratha_the_hidden_force_in _global_economics_sending_money_home?language=en

Schellekens, P. (2001). English Language as a Barrier to Employment, Education and Training. *Research Report* 4RP 210/98. Available at www.education.gov.uk

Sirkeci, I. (2009). Transnational mobility and conflict. *Migration Letters*, 6(1): 3-14.

Sirkeci, I. (2013). *Transnational Marketing and Transnational Consumers.* Springer, New York, Heidelberg, London.

Sirkeci, I. (2014). Globalisation is Over: The era of transnational marketing and connected consumers. *World Financial Review.* Available at http://www. worldfinancialreview.com/?p=645

Sirkeci, I. (2016). Would investing in financial literacy help reduce the use of informal channels? *People Move Blog*, The World Bank. Available at http://blogs.worldbank.

org/peoplemove/would-investing-financial-literacy-help-reduce-use-informal-channels

Sirkeci, I., & Cohen, J.H., & Ratha, D. (2012). *Migration and Remittances during the Global Financial Crisis and Beyond.* Washington, DC. US: The World Bank.

The Working Group on ESOL (2000). Breaking the Language Barriers. *The Report of the Working Group on English for Speakers of Other Languages (ESOL),* p.10. Available at www.lifelonglearning.co.uk

TRANSNATIONAL MARKETING JOURNAL

ISSN: 2041 4684
e-ISSN: 2041-4692

Abbreviated title: Transntl. Market. J.

Transnational Marketing Journal (TMJ) seeks to advance knowledge and contribute to the debates in Marketing. *Transnational Marketing Journal* is dedicated to publishing high quality contemporary research into transnational marketing practices and scholarship while encouraging critical approaches in the development of marketing theory and practice. *Transnational Marketing Journal* aims to publish high-quality papers on transnational marketing, the emphasis being on current interests, marketing practice and theory development. The journal offers an outlet for research and scholarship in this growing field in marketing research.

Transnational Marketing Journal is indexed and abstracted in:
China Academic Journals Database (CNKI Scholar)
Index Copernicus
EBSCO Academic Search international
EBSCO Business Source
Research Papers in Economics (RePEc)

Transnational Marketing Journal is published twice a year in May and October.

Transnational Marketing Journal is published by Transnational Press London, UK.

Addresses:
URL: www.transnationalmarket.com
Email: editor@transnationalmarket.com

ISSN: 2041-4684 (Print) - e-ISSN: 2041-4692 (Online)

Transnational Marketing Journal

Volume 4 - Number 1
May 2016

Transnational Marketing Journal

Manuscript submissions
Papers submitted should be original unpublished accounts of up to 8,000 words in length, excluding notes and references. Submissions must be written in English and should be submitted online.

For author guidelines, please visit the journal website. Opinions expressed in *Transnational Marketing Journal* are those of the authors and not necessarily those of the editors or publisher. Authors are personally responsible for obtaining permission for the reprint of previously published material.

Editorial Policy
All manuscripts are refereed by the associate editors and external reviewers. *Transnational Marketing Journal* follows a double-blind review policy. Referees are expected to provide supportive comments regarding their decisions. Following the receipt of a manuscript in the appropriate format, we anticipate a decision within three months.

Information for subscribers
Transnational Marketing Journal publishes 2 issues per annum in May and October. Current subscription prices are available on our website and by request via email at **sales@tplondon.com**.

Back issues
Current and recent volumes and issues are available for purchase. Please address such requests to:
> **sales@tplondon.com**

Advertisement
Any advertising requests should be addressed to:
> **sales@tplondon.com**

Web address: http://www.transnationalmarket.com

TRANSNATIONAL PRESS®
LONDON

Transnational Marketing Journal

Volume 3 - Number 2
October 2015

Transnational Marketing Journal

Volume 3 - Number 1
May 2015

www.ingramcontent.com/pod-product-compliance
Lightning Source LLC
Chambersburg PA
CBHW071126210326
41519CB00020B/6446